Original title:
The Meadow Speaks

Copyright © 2025 Creative Arts Management OÜ
All rights reserved.

Author: Miriam Kensington
ISBN HARDBACK: 978-1-80567-074-2
ISBN PAPERBACK: 978-1-80567-154-1

Nature's Gentle Murmur

The green grass giggles in the breeze,
Winking at daisies, oh what a tease!
Butterflies dance like they've lost their mind,
Chasing each other, what joy they find.

A squirrel declares, 'I'm the king of this tree!'
While birds chime in, 'You're just as silly as me!'
The flowers chatter, spilling all the seed,
Sharing gossip like it's the latest creed.

Voices of the Blossoms

Tulips whisper, 'We're dressed to impress,'
While roses roll their eyes, confess,
'Your colors are nice, but where's the flair?'
They switch their hats, pretend not to care.

Sunflowers laugh, 'We're the tallest around!'
While daisies shout, 'But we're cuter, we're crowned!'
The whole garden giggles, a floral delight,
In this patch of chaos, all feels just right.

The Language of the Leaves

Leaves gossip away, when the wind takes a break,
'Where's the breeze gone? We all need a shake!'
With rustles and whispers, they make quite the sound,
Chattering secrets that swirl all around.

Maple says, 'I'm fashionably late!'
While oak elbows pine, 'Don't sit and wait!'
From whispers to chuckles, the canopy's fun,
In leafy laughter, they bask in the sun.

Serenade of the Soft Soil

In the rich brown soil, worms start to sing,
'We're the underground crew, watch us spring!'
They wiggle and giggle, a squirmy parade,
While beetles tap dance, in soft earth they wade.

Moles comment, 'What a marvelous show!'
As roots hum along, in a rhythmic flow.
Earthworms unite, throwing a grand bash,
With soil like a stage, they all make a splash.

Reflections in the Meadow's Heart

In the field where daisies laugh,
Wear the sun like a silly scarf.
Butterflies gossip, what a show!
"Did you see that bee trip? Oh, no!"

The brook chuckles, waves hello,
Tickling rocks, putting on a show.
Frogs wear crowns of clover bright,
Croaking jokes under twilight's light.

Grasshoppers jump with flair and style,
One lost a shoe, but still, they smile.
With every leap, a splash of cheer,
As the wildflowers toss back their hair.

The Story of the Swaying Grasses

In the breeze, the grasses sway,
Holding a dance party, hip-hip-hooray!
They twirl and spin, grasshoppers cheer,
Even the cows wiggle their rear!

One clump bets who can stand straight,
But the wind just giggles, sealing their fate.
A tumble here, a bendy there,
Who knew fabric could have such flair?

And when the rain drizzles down,
They wear puddles like crowns, not a frown.
"Look at us!" the tall grasses boast,
"We're nature's funniest, let's raise a toast!

Songs of the Soaring Sky

Birds belt tunes with a cheeky twist,
"Catch me if you can!" they insist.
A crow drops a joke, lands with a thud,
While sparrows laugh, dancing in the mud.

Clouds fluff like pillows drifting high,
One white puff shouts, "I'm the sly guy!"
Hiccups in the air, a wind-serenade,
Kites join in, parading and played.

Bees buzz bass notes, quite out of tune,
As critters gather, it's their festoon.
Songs float down, through leaves they weave,
Nature's concert, hard to believe!

Dialogue of the Dancing Shadows

Shadows shimmy under the tree,
"Who stepped on my toe?" says one with glee.
They stretch and bounce at the sun's decree,
Swaying like dancers, wild and free.

"Let's split for a joke!" one tiptoes away,
"I'm off to prank a nearby ray!"
Laughter echoes through the grass so tall,
As shadows tumble like a silly ball.

"Who knows how to do the moonlight glide?"
One whispers low, filled with pride.
A flare of laughter, shadows entwined,
In daylight's end, they aren't hard to find.

On the Edge of Every Flower

Petals gossip, they love to tease,
Buzzing bees share the latest breeze.
A ladybug rolls, with elegance in sight,
Flaunting spots like fashion, oh what a delight!

Sunshine chuckles, a playful glow,
Tickling grass blades, putting on a show.
The butterfly winks, flutters with flair,
In this garden jest, no worries to bear.

Segments of Solitude and Beauty

Dandelions dream, a wish on the air,
Making a wish? Well, I wouldn't dare!
They puff out their seeds, like tiny balloons,
Floating away, like nature's cartoons.

A squirrel dashes, a nut in his paws,
Pausing to ponder, then slips on green moss.
He snickers at shadows, the jokes on the run,
In this quiet corner, oh what fun!

Whispering Threads of Life's Fabric

Threads of cobweb shiver with grace,
Spider spins stories, a delicate lace.
With every tiny step, the critters confide,
In this vibrant tapestry, joy cannot hide.

A worm tells tales of the soil's embrace,
Dancing in circles, with such silly grace.
The grasshoppers chirp, a tune to unwind,
In life's simple fabric, laughter you'll find.

The Choreography of Nature's Dance

The wind sways the trees, a whimsical waltz,
  Leaves flutter and giggle, as if at a fault.
  A rabbit hops in, with moves so absurd,
Stumbling and tumbling, you'd think it a bird!

Crickets keep time with their nightly refrain,
  Their serenade echoes, a sweet, silly gain.
  Nature's own stage holds a comical spree,
  Where laughter unveils, and joy runs free.

Unwritten Notes in the Morning Dew

In the grass, the dew drops dance,
Whispering secrets, given a chance.
A ladybug with a silly grin,
Tells the world, 'Come on, let's spin!'

Curious ants with tiny hats,
Debate on whether to chase down cats.
The sun peeks in, a little shy,
While butterflies wave their 'hello' fly!

Ballads of the Flourishing Realms

Squirrels sing with nuts in hand,
A chorus of chaos, perfectly planned.
The daisies giggle, jiggling about,
As rabbits join in, hopping with clout.

A frog strums a leaf, a fiddle so fine,
Croaking rhythm, keeping time.
The breezes laugh, swaying the trees,
While bees wear sunglasses, buzzing with ease.

Tuning into the Wild Heartbeat

Rabbits thump their feet in time,
To a woodpecker's rhythmic rhyme.
The flowers sway, they're in the zone,
Cooking up giggles, a joyful tone.

A snail races, oh what a sight!
Pacing with purpose, oh what a fight!
The crickets chirp in delightful strains,
While a blushing rose flirts with the plains.

Reflections of Nature's Pulse

The sun winks down while shadows play,
As frolicsome frogs leap in the fray.
Wind tickles leaves with a cheeky laugh,
While daisies plot a flowered gaffe.

A caterpillar with dreams so grand,
Jokes with the clouds, merging like sand.
Nature chuckles, a hearty cheer,
In this wild realm, joy's always near!

Symphony of the Sunlit Glade

In a glade where squirrels dance,
They invite a bird to prance.
The trees hum a silly tune,
Underneath the laughing moon.

Bumblebees wear tiny hats,
Chasing butterflies and chats.
A frog leaps with a joyful croak,
While rabbits joke with every poke.

The daisies all dance in line,
Swaying, sipping sunshine wine.
A hedgehog jokes with a sly grin,
As the laughter starts to spin.

Lullabies of the Land

Grasshoppers sing with a buzz,
While the ants parade just because.
A turtle drags its little feet,
And claims it runs like lightning fleet.

The daisies giggle, oh so bright,
Tickling worms with pure delight.
A snail, determined, takes its chance,
Yet loses track and starts to prance.

Under clouds that are fluffy and grand,
Nature's chorus makes a cool band.
The wind whispers a tickling tune,
As giggles echo 'neath the moon.

The Poetry of Petals

Petals toss in the summer air,
Making stunts without a care.
A bumblebee plays peek-a-boo,
While daisies shout, "Look at us too!"

Lilies giggle from their pond,
While frogs play music, of which they're fond.
Every bloom's a little star,
Telling stories, raising the bar.

In the dance of colors, oh so bright,
Flora tumble, causing mild fright.
With every rustle, laughter weaves,
As nature crafts its fun reprieves.

Melodies of the Moonlit Space

At nighttime, critters have a ball,
In moonlit fields, they heed the call.
A raccoon juggling acorns, spry,
While the owls wink and flutter by.

Crickets play their nightly jam,
While a skunk dreams of glam and slam.
Fireflies join in with a glow,
Making the show a bright tableau.

A raccoon with a stolen pie,
Dances with glee, oh my, oh my!
As the stars look down with a wink,
Nature's stage in laughter's sync.

The Rhythms of Root and Wing

In the soil a worm did wiggle,
Singing songs that made us giggle.
The birds on high took up the tune,
Dancing wildly 'neath the moon.

A squirrel jumped with such a flair,
Claiming all the nuts to share.
But when they fell, oh what a scene,
A nutty ruckus, quite routine!

Harmonies in the Humming Hive

Buzzing bees in a silly race,
Chasing pollen, oh what a chase!
Their tiny wings create a buzz,
But all they want is sweetened fuzz.

A ladybug joins in the fray,
Dressed in spots, she steals the display.
Spinning tales with every glide,
A tiny diva, full of pride!

Nature's Artistry in Motion

A rabbit painted on a tree,
With colors bright, quite twisty-free.
He chuckled loud, "I'm an artist too!"
While trying to hop and stretch anew.

The flowers giggled in the breeze,
Swapping petals with utmost ease.
A dandelion, quite bold and spry,
Declared, "Watch my seeds, they fly!"

Sagas of Serene Stillness

A turtle sat, thinking quite deep,
Dreaming of fast, while others leap.
"Slow and steady wins the day,"
He chuckled softly, with a sway.

The pond reflected a fishy grin,
Splashing joy, oh what a win!
With belly flops and leaps so grand,
Acrobats of the waterland!

Tales of the Ground Beneath

A worm wore a hat, quite absurd,
While ants wrote a play, yes, they stirred.
The clover looked up, quite befuddled,
At the grasshopper's dance, all a muddle.

With roots that can tickle and tease,
The daisies conspired to bring you to knees.
"Oh, will you not stay?" the dandelions croon,
While the beetle just chuckled, under the moon.

The gopher threw parties, inviting the beet,
But everyone knows he can't dance on his feet.
A chorus of crickets with songs filled with cheer,
Claimed they were the stars of this lively frontier.

So down in the soil, in a world so bizarre,
The laughter erupts, it's a comedy bar.
Each creature has tales, oh, what a delight,
Just don't ask the mole, he'll be home for the night.

Reverie of the Wandering Clouds

The clouds played dress-up, all fluff and flair,
One shaped like a cat, the others a bear.
They drifted and danced in a breezy parade,
While sunbeams applauded, sunlight, their trade.

"Oh look, a lion!" one cloud squealed in mirth,
"A plethora of creatures, all born from the girth!"
The wind laughed so hard, it spun 'round a tree,
And whispered to flowers, "Join in with me."

But raindrops held grudges, they wanted to fall,
They pouted and shouted, demanding a call.
"Let's brighten this circus, let's do something grand,
I'd love to perform, help us splash on the land!"

With each drop of joy, the blooms began twirl,
The whole sky erupted, in petals they swirled.
A comedy show up in the skies above,
Filled with fluffy antics and clouds full of love.

Soundscapes of the Rural Heart

The rooster crowed loud, "I'm the dawn's own king!"
While the cows chimed in, with their mooing bling.
Farm dogs juggled bones, oh what a sight,
As pigs pratfall danced, with sheer delight.

The scarecrow spoke jokes, quite witty, you see,
Dropping punchlines, amidst the corn spree.
"Why don't we race? I'm slower than slow,"
The rabbit replied with a confident glow.

Then turkeys rehearsed for Thanksgiving's grand show,
With feathers all fluffed, putting on quite the glow.
"Let's waddle and shimmy, let's strut with some flair,"
While the farmer just chuckled, shaking his hair.

Oh, this rural heart beats with laughter and cheer,
A symphony of antics that all creatures hear.
So raise up your glass, to the farm's funny scene,
Where every day's punchline is quirky and keen.

The Narrative Thread of Wild Grasses

The grass whispered tales in rustling tones,
Of beetles who dreamed of building fine homes.
"We'll make it of clover, with plush velvet floors,"
The butterflies giggled, mapping out doors.

With each gentle sway, the stories took flight,
Of ants who believed they could conquer the night.
"Let's form a parade with our tiny parade,"
While the spiders just chuckled, "We're well overlaid."

The willy-nilly wind joined the charade,
With whispers of gossip from shade to the glade.
"Have you heard the one 'bout the mouse and the cat?"
"Oh do tell it again, that's a real tit-for-tat!"

The grasses laughed loud, their laughter so sweet,
They tangled in tales, as they waltzed with feet.
Together they wove a narrative bright,
Under the sun's glow, from morning till night.

Tales Told by the Tall Pines

Tall pines whisper secrets, full of cheer,
They joke with the squirrels who scamper near.
"Did you hear the one about the wobbly bee?"
"He danced on a blossom, fell right into tea!"

With branches a-dancing and needles so bright,
They chuckle at shadows that creep in the night.
"Why did the rabbit hop over the log?"
"To avoid the debate with a wise old frog!"

Their laughter resounds through the rustling leaves,
As gossip flows freely, it never deceives.
"Last week the crows threw a big feathered bash,
But the owls showed up and made quite a smash!"

Each breeze carries tales of the silly, sublime,
Nature's comedians, lost in their rhyme.
With giggles and grins, they sway to the song,
In the forest of laughter, you'll never go wrong.

Harmony in the Hum of Insects

Insects are buzzing, creating a tune,
Bees bumble along, in a hive of buffoon.
A caterpillar said, "I'll be a butterfly!"
A cricket replied, "Sure, but who'll ask you why?"

The ants march in step, a parade of the small,
"Who needs a GPS? We're experts, after all!"
With tiny smartphones they plan their great trek,
But all ends in chaos, what a hectic wreck!

Grasshoppers laugh as they leap through the air,
"Did you catch that last joke? Come on, don't you dare!"
They chirp and they chatter, creating a scene,
Even ladybugs giggle, oh, how they preen!

In this buzzing bazaar, humor hums all around,
Nature's own chorus, joyfully profound.
With mischief and missteps, they glide with such style,
Insects and laughter walk that extra mile.

The Chorus of the Verdant Field

Fields open wide with a carpet of green,
Where daisies and dandelions play hide and glean.
"What's a flower's favorite game?" asked the clover,
"Hide and seek! But that's only when it's over!"

Tall grasses sway, making faces galore,
Whispering secrets like never before.
"A worm told me once that he learned to tango!"
"Then let's start a dance-off, oh, what a show!"

Chirpy little robins pitch in with a song,
"Join our tune of the day, we'll all sing along!"
But the doggone crickets strummed out of key,
"They've stolen the spotlight, can you believe me?"

With blushing petals and giggling stems,
Nature's own performers, oh, how it transcends!
In the theater of greens, laughter springs free,
While the sun sets the stage for all that will be.

Murmurs of the Morning Dew

Morning dew gathers, glistening bright,
Each droplet a jewel, a marvelous sight.
"What's the dew say to the sun every day?"
"Don't melt me too early; I'd like to stay!"

Tiny droplets gather, as gossip unfolds,
"I've heard the wind's stories, some daring, some bold!"
A drop named Dewdrop shouted with glee,
"Let's trick the flowers to dance! One, two, three!"

As the sun rises up, with a wink and a tease,
The grasses start shaking, rustling in the breeze.
"Was that a joke? Or did I just dream?"
"No, it's just the birds singing sweet with a beam!"

So they twinkle and shimmer, a playful affair,
Nature's own diamonds, they float through the air.
The morning brings laughter, as dawn breaks anew,
And the world starts to giggle, bright under the dew.

Secrets Beneath the Wildflowers

The daisies gossip, oh so bright,
Sharing tales from dawn till night.
"I saw a bee trip on a dot,"
"Not cool, my dear, but that's his lot!"

A ladybug rolled, quite full of cheer,
Sipping nectar, never fear.
"Did you hear about the grass so tall?,"
"Stood up to the wind, almost took a fall!"

Buttercups laugh at the sun's warm glow,
"Told the clouds, 'Just take it slow!'
But they raced by, causing a fuss,
Making puddles, oh, what a bust!"

With secrets swaying in the breeze,
Nature's whispers bring us to our knees.
So listen closely when you roam,
Wildflowers share quirks of their home!

A Symphony of Rustling Leaves

In the trees, a band begins to play,
Leaves flapping arms, hip-hip-hooray!
A squirrel's solo, a leap and a twirl,
"Look at me dance," he gives a whirl!

Crisp sounds echo, a rustling choir,
"Can you hear us? We never tire!"
A gust comes in, a big ol' tease,
"Don't get too loud, we'll shake the leaves!"

A bumblebee buzzes, ready to jive,
"Did you see? I felt so alive!"
With a wiggle and wobble, flutter and spin,
Leaves let out giggles, "Let the fun begin!"

The branches sway to a woodland beat,
Nature's dance, oh, isn't it sweet?
In vibrant bursts, both high and low,
Under the sky, their laughter flows.

Voices from the Rustic Patch

In the rustic patch, the pumpkins grin,
"Who's the guest? Is it time to win?"
A scarecrow chuckles, wide-brimmed hat,
"Everyone's welcome, even that cat!"

Carrots whisper of their deep, dark roots,
"Think the chef knows we're such hoots?"
They dream of being in soup or stew,
But chuckle at what they might go through.

Radishes pout, a bit self-aware,
"Red like a rose, but none seem to care!"
Yet the herbs just laugh, oh so spry,
"Don't you know? You're the star of the fry!"

In this patch of giggles and cheer,
Every critter holds stories dear.
From squashes bold to beans galore,
Voices blend, oh, who could ask for more?

Conversations Amongst the Daisies

Daisies chatter, "What's your hue today?"
"Bright as the sun!" "Mine's a bit gray."
They share their quirks, secrets unfold,
"Last week, I sported a petal of gold!"

A fellow flower, a shy little bud,
"Did I hear right? Oh, what a stud!"
Bumbling bees buzz, "Did you try the cake?"
"Just pollen fluff, for goodness' sake!"

"You should join in, wear your best hat!"
"I'm happy as I am, imagine that!"
Laughter rings out, soft in the air,
Encouraging words, they bloom without care.

As sunbeams dance and shadows sway,
In this patch of laughter, the flowers play.
Each petal a story, every stem a laugh,
In their delight, they share the path.

Whispers of the Wild Grass

In the field where the wild grass sways,
The dandelions flirt in sunny rays.
They giggle at bugs, so clumsy and slow,
While ants in a line march to and fro.

A rabbit hops by, with style and grace,
Wearing a crown made of daisies, what a face!
The grass whispers secrets, oh what a jest,
As the wind joins in, putting them to the test.

A squirrel jokes loudly, with acorns galore,
He drops one on purpose; the crowd wants more!
Chasing and laughing, the critters all play,
While the wild grasses sway in a whimsical way.

Just listen closely, shh, can you hear?
The grass has a rumor that tickles the ear.
Each rustle and laugh in this vibrant dance,
Turns the mundane into pure, silly chance.

Echoes Beneath the Sun

Underneath the sun, the shadows prance,
Grasshoppers sing, they love to dance.
"Catch me if you can!" they laugh and they leap,
While butterflies swarm in a colorful heap.

A snail tells a tale of the world he explored,
His adventures so grand, and yet, he's ignored.
"Slow and steady wins the race," he insists,
But the rabbit just yawned, and off he did twist!

The sun smiles down on this lively scene,
As flowers throw petals like confetti, so keen.
Each breeze tells a joke that we'll surely miss,
A comedy show in the summer's bliss.

So come join the echoes of laughter and cheer,
Where the wild things play through each shady sphere.
Nature's big stage, where whimsy's a must,
Leaving us in giggles, and laughter's sweet trust.

Conversations with the Daisies

Daisies are chattering, "Did you hear the news?"
They talk about raindrops and their favorite shoes.
"I prefer the puddles," said one with a grin,
"And I love the breeze that cools me within!"

"Yesterday, a butterfly thought I was a plate!"
They giggle and chatter, it's a funny fate.
A ladybug rolls, and they all break a laugh,
As she accidentally joins the daisies' staff.

"Do you smell that cake?" a daisy did hum,
"Oh wait, that's just pollen, not sweet like a crumb!"
Still, the daisies sing with glee all around,
Making sure all their humor and joy can be found.

So if you walk by, bend down for a peek,
You'll hear their sweet laughter, a whimsical squeak.
Nature's own merry, in bloom and in jest,
The daisies will always give laughter their best.

Secrets in the Breeze

The breeze carries whispers, both funny and bright,
   Of squirrels with acorns planning their flight.
"Did you see the owl?" a mouse squeaks with glee,
   "He winked at the sun, down here, by the tree!"

A butterfly flutters with dreams in her eyes,
   "Last week, I danced with the clouds in the skies!"
While grasses giggle, their blades in a row,
   As they shake and shimmy, putting on quite a show.

The wind plays the jester, so light and so free,
   Telling tales of the rabbit who lost his key.
A riddle from nature, a giggle ensued,
   As a frog croaked along, quite puzzled but glued.

In this playful kingdom, where laughter ignites,
   The secrets of nature bring joy and delights.
So listen, dear friend, to the wind's funny tune,
   For in every breath, there's a chuckle by noon.

Autumn's Canvas of Rustling Dream

Leaves twirl like dancers in flight,
Chasing the breeze, what a sight!
Squirrels chatter, their acorn heist,
Planning a feast for the winter's feast.

Pumpkins grinning, quite the scene,
Winking at folks, what a routine!
Scarecrows posing, striking a stance,
Whispering secrets of harvest romance.

Reflective Thoughts of the Verdant Realm

Grass tickles toes in playful glee,
While ants march on their grand spree.
A wise old owl hoots out a riddle,
While mockingbirds play a tune, oh so middle!

Dandelions puff and blow them away,
They're in on the joke, come what may!
A whispering brook chuckles at the sun,
Saying, 'Stay a while, oh, isn't this fun?'

The Hidden Treasures of Flora

Bumblebees buzzing like tiny planes,
Racing each other, ignoring the rains.
Petals don hats of the brightest hue,
Looking for gossip like flowers do!

Mushrooms having a tea party so sly,
With ladybugs chatting, oh my, oh my!
They sip from dew drops, share tales quite absurd,
While telling secrets in whispers unheard.

The Ode of Softening Light

Sunset spills gold across the field,
While shadows play, their secrets revealed.
Crickets strum tunes on a violin's string,
Inviting the moon for a moonlit fling!

Fireflies flash like fairy lights,
Dancing with joy in the fading sights.
The jokes of twilight, a giggle or two,
As the stars peek in, and the night bids adieu.

The Soliloquy of the Swaying Ferns

In a dance with the breeze, they sway with glee,
Ferns gossiping secrets, who'll hear their decree?
"Did you see that squirrel? Oh, the tricks he pulls!"
"I heard he thinks he's cooler than us, what a fool!"

With the sunlight's tickle, they blush ever bright,
"Oh, look at that butterfly! Is it lost in flight?"
"Such a show-off, it flits, flaunting colors so bold,"
"But we've got style too, our greens never grow old!"

They whisper of rain, a sweet pitter-patter,
"Look at the daisies! They're all in a chatter!"
"Bet they think they're the stars of the floral parade,"
"Little do they know, we'll dance when they fade!"

So sway they may, but they've wisdom to share,
In laughter and chatter, no fern's ever bare.
Each flounce, each rustle, it's life's little jest,
In the garden of giggles, they're living their best!

Serenade of the Wandering Breeze

Oh, how I love to tease the trees,
A little rustle here, a tickle with ease.
"Catch me if you can!" I call to the leaves,
But they just laugh back, as if they're the thieves!

Pondering where to blow next, oh what a thrill!
Through flowers and tall grass, I take my sweet fill.
"Do you think they know I'm the king of the air?"
"They're too busy buzzing; they hardly would care!"

As I wander through gardens and giggle with glee,
I swoop down to whisper to old Mr. Bee.
"Do you think it's my charm that makes flowers sway?"
"Maybe it's your perfume—and I don't mean 'hay'!"

At dusk I'll retreat, with tales full of cheer,
The laughter of petals, I hold so dear.
As the world quiets down, they beg me to stay,
But I'm a wandering breeze, forever in play!

Requiem of the Retiring Clouds

The clouds are having quite a farewell show,
"Did you see that rainbow? Come, let's steal the glow!"
"Who knew that rain could bring such cheer?"
"Only when wrapped in colors, we shed no tear!"

They puff out their chests, as if strutting away,
"Time for our nap, we've worked hard all day!"
With a yawn and a stretch, they begin to disperse,
"Onward to dreams, who wants the next verse?"

But the sun peeks through, saying, "Not so fast!"
"You clouds look too cozy, don't make this a blast!"
"Come join our fun, let's play hide and seek!"
"Oh please, dear sunshine, we just want to peek!"

So they linger a while, in a playful embrace,
But soon their soft sighs signal it's time to race.
With laughter and puffs, they drift out of sight,
Clouds fading like whispers, goodnight, dear twilight!

Chants from the Evening Glow

As dusk blankets fields, the glow starts to hum,
Creatures gather 'round, for the evening's fun!
"Have you heard the crickets? They've got quite the tune!"
"And the fireflies dance, like sparks in the gloom!"

The moon joins the party, a silvery guest,
"What's that, little bumblebee? Ready to rest?"
"Not yet," he buzzes, "tonight's still ablaze!"
"With all of you here, I'm in a sweet maze!"

Grass blades quarrel softly, over who's the best,
"I sway with more flair, compared to the rest!"
"But without me here, would you even exist?"
"Oh grass, we're a team, regret not this twist!"

As the shadows deepen and laughter takes flight,
The glow carries on, until the stars are in sight.
In the last bursts of joy, the night does unfold,
Chants of the evening, where magic is gold!

The Language of the Greenlands

In the grass, the rabbits gossip,
While the daisies dance and sway.
The snails tell secrets—oh so slow,
And the ants hold a grand buffet.

A squirrel chuckles at a crow's call,
As they argue over shiny things.
The flowers a-buzz with pollen jokes,
While the wind plays silly strings.

The earthworms wiggle in delight,
Singing of squishy, muddy trails.
The sunbeams giggle and tickle the grass,
As butterflies share their tales.

So listen close and take a seat,
Join this green and lively crew.
Where laughter flows beneath the trees,
And everything's just a bit askew.

Stories of the Sunlit Knoll

Oh, the sunlit knoll is full of cheer,
With crickets providing the tunes.
The ladybugs laugh as they spin around,
While the bees play peek-a-boo with the moons.

The frogs are sporting tiny crowns,
Croaking loudly, 'We're the kings!'
The butterflies flutter and tease them back,
As the whole meadow happily sings.

In the shadows, a clever fox waits,
With a story—quite grand, he claims.
But the mice in the grass just roll their eyes,
And say, 'We prefer cheese, not games.'

So gather round for a merry time,
Where the stories are silly and grand.
In the sunlit knoll, joy is infectious,
And laughter is never quite banned.

Murmurs in the Blissful Breeze

Whispers in the air bring giggles anew,
As the trees share puns with each other.
The wind blows softly, carrying tales,
Of a snail who was once a speedy brother.

With each rustle, the leaves break out,
In fits of laughter, don't you see?
The flowers sway, pondering if,
They could ever be as funny as the bee.

The clouds above join in the fun,
Playing tag, then tickling the sun.
While shadows dance, making faces,
In this world where there's always a pun.

So let the breeze lift your spirits higher,
As you trot through this playful land.
For here every whisper is full of jest,
And joy is scattered like grains of sand.

Rhythms of Nature's Choir

In the meadow, a chorus begins,
With frogs and crickets on the stage.
Butterflies flit, adding their flair,
While the daisies giggle, freeing the cage.

The clouds hum low, the sun beams bright,
They all join in a merry tune.
Even the ants march to the beat,
As the grass tickles them like a cartoon.

And what's a show without some pranks?
The raven jokes at the fox's expense.
While the flowers clap their petal hands,
Cheering for nature's fun commence.

So dance along with the swaying trees,
As laughter and joy fill the air.
For in this choir of merry notes,
Every heart will find that laughter is rare.

The Call of the Clouds Above

Up above the world so wide,
Fluffy shapes in blue reside.
One's a dog, I think I see,
Chasing tails of breeze and glee.

Whispers tickle as they float,
Hats and shoes they seem to gloat.
"Catch us if you think you can!"
They giggle like a playful fan.

Sunbeams dance and tease their friends,
As shadows stretch and make amends.
A cloud-napper on a lazy day,
Dreaming of a light-hearted play.

But wait! Is that a raindrop's plan?
A game of splashes, oh, how grand!
Through puddles deep, we'll take a leap,
And laugh like kids, no need for sleep.

A Tapestry of Dappled Light

Sunlight weaves with shadows tight,
A patchwork quilt, oh what a sight!
Dandelions dance upon the floor,
Like sprightly dancers, who could ask for more?

A squirrel prances, top hat askew,
While grasshoppers plan a ball for two.
They jump and jig on leafy stage,
As butterflies flip through every page.

Rays peek through with a wink and grin,
Playing hide and seek, oh where to begin?
The flowers nod like actors proud,
Performing for a lively crowd.

A leaf falls down, joins the fun,
Rolling 'round, it laughs on the run.
Nature's merriment, what a show,
In this dappled light, let joy overflow!

Whispers of Verdant Grace

The grass hums a quirky tune,
As ants march out to meet the moon.
A rabbit hops, he stops to chat,
Sharing secrets with a sleeping cat.

In corners green, the flowers giggle,
While bees with tiny wigs just wiggle.
They gather 'round for tea and chat,
Discussing life, like that and that!

Mice in coats of royal blue,
Hold court, announcing jesters too.
With every squeak, they break the ice,
In fields of green, who needs a vice?

A breeze brings tales from far away,
Of creatures bold and shows of play.
In verdant realms where laughter starts,
Nature's voice can win our hearts.

Echoes in the Tall Grass

In tall grass where echoes come to play,
Grasshoppers cheer, bounce, and sway.
Crickets sing in a band of four,
As daisies poke fun and ask for more.

A raccoon joins in with a funny hat,
Swaying like he's lost his bat!
He twirls and spins, a sight indeed,
Flipping over roots at lightning speed.

Gentle whispers weave through the breeze,
Tickling leaf tips, dancing with ease.
Laughter spills like raindrops, bright,
In the green expanse, all feels right.

So come and hear the mirthful sound,
Where echoes bounce and joy abounds.
In the tall grass, let spirits grow,
And frolic where the laughter flows.

Messages Carried by the Wind

Whispers dance through grass and glade,
Telling tales of the pranks they've made.
A squirrel chuckles, chasing its tail,
While frogs on lily pads tell a tall tale.

The gusts play tricks like a friendly ghost,
Making shy bumblebees run from their post.
A dandelion puff floats like a joke,
Spreading laughter with every poke.

The breeze is gossip, swirling with flair,
Knock-knock jokes vanish in sweet air.
As crickets chirp their midnight tunes,
The wind howls back like a fool that croons.

Oh, listen close to nature's delight,
With rhymes and giggles, the world feels bright.
Each breeze a comedian in leafy disguise,
Tickling our senses as it glides by.

Elysian Echoes at Twilight

Evening descends with a chuckle and wink,
As shadows stretch out, the crickets link.
Fireflies blink like stars with a jest,
While frogs in the bog wear their best vest.

The twilight giggles, a sight to behold,
As whispers of laughter in violet unfold.
Hares hop and tumble, they're late to the show,
While owls in the oaks nod off in a row.

The evening breeze plays hopscotch with leaves,
Crafting a riddle that nobody believes.
Each whispering echo is a tale in itself,
More cherished than treasures stacked high on a shelf.

As night wraps around like a cozy old quilt,
The chuckles of twilight, a joyous kilt.
In the garden's embrace, we share in the bliss,
For nature's two cents is one sweet, silly kiss.

Rhapsody of the Untamed

In fields wild and free, chaos does reign,
Where roses chat back and thistles complain.
A hedgehog rolls over, a real funny sight,
While daisies gossip about fashion at night.

The dandelions whisper, 'We're not weeds, dear!'
'We're puffs of sunshine with nothing to fear!'
While the poppies parade in their bright, frilly gowns,
Grasshoppers hop, wearing imaginary crowns.

An owl gives a hoot, but not out of fright,
He's just making sure that all's feeling right.
With a hiccup, the creek sings its merry old tune,
As fireflies join in, flickering like the moon.

The grasses sway, doing a giggling dance,
While twirly vines curl, entranced in their prance.
Amidst nature's follies, joy takes its stage,
In this rhapsody wild, life's humor's the page.

The Silent Storyteller of Flora

Among the blooms where laughter is sown,
A flower plots mischief, not one is alone.
Petals unfold, spilling secrets so bright,
While stems stretch and sway, preparing for flight.

A sunflower beams with a grin that's so wide,
As it throws a wink at the bees zipped inside.
Breezes carry tales of silly past days,
Where daffodils dance in the sun's golden rays.

The violets hum tunes of blunders and gags,
Entwining with ivy that playfully drags.
Every leaf has a story, every root adds a quip,
In the garden of laughter, sip after sip.

'Tis true that silence often speaks volumes,
As flora shares secrets with gentle costumes.
In the quiet corners, funny tales bloom,
Where whispers of nature chase away gloom.

Chronicle of the Buzzing Bees

In flowers bright, they dance with glee,
With tiny wigs, as busy bees.
They laugh and hum, oh what a sight,
Stealing nectar morning, noon, and night.

A bee once slipped, and fell on a shoe,
"Honey, help! I'm stuck like glue!"
The flower chuckled, swayed with cheer,
"Just bumble on, my dear, no fear!"

One bee took flight, too much to drink,
He zigged and zagged, then paused to think.
"Maybe next time, I'll sip with care,
Or dance like crazy, in the air."

So buzzing friends, they prance and play,
In this sweet life, they find their way.
They toast to blooms, both big and small,
In their honeyed world, they love it all.

The Tranquil Serenade of Nature

The trees whisper secrets, oh so sly,
While squirrels plot schemes to steal and fly.
The birds hold court, with songs in the air,
While ants march on, without a care.

A rabbit stopped, to smell a rose,
"A perfect snack!" he brightly chose.
But thorns sprang up, "No munching here!"
He hopped away, "I'll stick to beer!"

The frogs croak jokes, by the moonlit pond,
Making all the crickets sing and respond.
"Why did the chicken cross?" one asked with a grin,
"To avoid the pond!" we all joined in.

In nature's concert, laughter takes flight,
With creatures united, day and night.
They dance to the rhythm, a merry show,
Where every rustle prompts a giggling flow.

Embrace of the Rolling Hills

On hills so round, the cows do roam,
One wears a hat, pretending to be Rome.
"Miss Moo, oh dear, you look so grand!"
"Just mixing style with clover brand!"

The sheep play tag, and race on by,
With woolly coats, they bounce and fly.
"Fat chance we lose!" they giggle with glee,
"Unless it rains and weighs down our spree!"

A pig rolled down; he thought it cool,
"Life's a blast when you're near the pool!"
But mud was slick, and whoosh he went,
"Next time I'll stick to the comfy tent!"

So on these hills, where laughter blooms,
Each creature adds to nature's tunes.
An embrace of mirth, as bright as the sun,
Rolling with joy, oh what fun!

Vibrations of the Open Space

In the open space, the wind plays loud,
Turning shy squirrels into a crowd.
"Who can jump highest?" they boldly shout,
Messy landings leave no doubt!

A grasshopper struts, his legs a show,
"Tap dance, everyone! Let's go, let's go!"
But tripped on a leaf, he took a spill,
"Next time I'll stick to the stillness, chill!"

The sun beams down, the laughter swells,
While flowers gossip, sharing their spells.
"Did you hear that bee? He's lost his groove!"
"Maybe his wings need a smooth move!"

So in this place, with joy abound,
Life bounces back in every sound.
With giggles echoing, a splendid race,
In the harmony of this bright, open space.

Oscillations of Color and Sound

In a field where daisies dance,
The ants are hosting a grand romance.
A butterfly flits with a swish,
While crickets serve up their best dish.

The sun beams down with a cheeky grin,
Birds sing tunes that make you spin.
Colors clash in a whimsical fight,
Making rainbows jealous of their sight.

The grass tickles toes in a playful tease,
While squirrels chitter with the greatest ease.
The flowers giggle as they sway,
In a meadow where antics rule the day.

A dog rolls by with a gleeful bark,
Chasing shadows 'til it gets dark.
Friendships bloom in this vibrant space,
Where joy and laughter interlace.

Whims of the Playful Wind

Oh the wind, with its silly prance,
Twists the leaves in a raucous dance.
It tickles noses, ruffles hair,
And plays tag with clouds without a care.

A kite goes flying, only to fall,
As the wind giggles and alters its call.
It whispers secrets to squirrels nearby,
While pushing dandelions into the sky.

The trees sway like they're having a ball,
Their branches waving as if to enthrall.
A breeze runs by, and whoosh, what a sound!
It's nature's laughter, all around.

With every gust, the world takes flight,
Creating chaos, pure delight.
In a field where whimsy abounds,
The playful wind shows off its sounds.

The Spoken Dreams of Blossoms

Blossoms chat in colors bright,
Sharing dreams that take to flight.
A rose tells tales of love's sweet kiss,
While daisies giggle, "We can't miss!"

Tulips argue who's the best dressed,
In their flamboyant gowns, they jest.
The violets nod, quite serene,
With whispers of mischief that are unseen.

A bumblebee buzzes with gossip in tow,
As petals lean in for the show.
They speak of pollen and sunny rays,
And how to make the most of their days.

Petal parties bloom in the glow,
With the fragrance of laughter in tow.
In this garden where dreams ignite,
The whispers of blossoms take flight.

Chronicles of the Sun and Soil

In the soil where secrets hide,
The worms compose tales with pride.
The sun grins wide, casting rays,
While plants join in a merry praise.

Little sprouts tell tales of yore,
Of rains and sun that they adore.
They stretch their leaves for a big high five,
In this storybook garden, alive!

The sun starts laughing, "I'm never shy!
Watch me glow, oh my, oh my!"
Flowers bloom, a vibrant crowd,
Cheering for daylight, humming loud.

Roots whisper low as they dig deep,
While shadows linger and secrets keep.
In this saga of bright and dark,
Life unfolds with a joyous spark.

Chronicles from the Meadow's Edge

In a field where daisies dance,
A squirrel tries to woo a prance.
He spins and twirls with quite a flair,
While bunnies giggle, unaware.

A butterfly with grand ideals,
Wears colors bright as banana peels.
It flutters by, so proud and neat,
Chasing ants who scamper on their feet.

The old oak tree, a gossip queen,
Whispers tales of snacks unseen.
Like bread crumbs dropped for birds at play,
Then complains about the heat of day.

The sun winks down, a cheeky twirl,
As grasshoppers play hop, twist, and swirl.
With every leap, a laugh escapes,
In this wild world of silly shapes.

The Calm Pulse of Nature's Breath

With every breeze, a ticklish tease,
The flowers giggle, shake with ease.
They sway together, wearing crowns,
While clouds above wear silly frowns.

A lazy snail takes all its time,
While rabbits race, oh what a crime!
But in the grass, they stop and stare,
At dusty bees who can't quite share.

A frog in mud sings out a joke,
While ladybugs in laughter choke.
They roll around, what silly fun,
Until they're off, all one by one.

In this odd land, no sense of stress,
Each critter knows just how to jest.
And when the moons begin to peep,
They whisper secrets before they sleep.

Echoes of Lives Unseen and Known

In shadows deep, the mice will plot,
To steal a crumb, oh what a lot!
They snicker low, but oh so brave,
The picnic basket is their grave.

A hedgehog rolls, a prickly ball,
While crickets laugh and start to crawl.
They play a tune that lifts the heart,
As fireflies join the nighttime art.

As the twilight paints the scene so bright,
Raccoons come out, what a sight!
With masks of black, they look so grand,
Robbers of treats from nature's hand.

The night unfolds with silly chats,
As owls hoot jokes and dance with bats.
Every critter knows the score,
In this wild life, there's always more!

Verses Carved in Mossy Ground

Beneath the trees, the roots entwine,
And mushrooms giggle, feeling fine.
The soil hums with stories bold,
Of dreams unshared and laughter gold.

A rabbit hops, then trips and slips,
And all around erupts in quips.
The sun peeks through in bursts of rays,
Witness to all the frolic plays.

A curious fox with eyes so bright,
Sneaks up to plot a little fright.
But roly-poly bugs just laugh,
And roll on by, a clever half.

As evening falls, the fireflies blink,
And crickets find their rhythm, sync.
In every crack, in every nook,
The forest holds a funny book.

Meditations on Petals and Breeze

In the grove, a flower sneezes,
Pollen wafts, the bee just teases.
A daisy giggles, short and bright,
While daisies dance under sunlight.

The tulips gossip, oh so bold,
About the sun and tales retold.
Caterpillars play hopscotch, too,
As grasshoppers croon a tune or two.

A dandelion, proud and spry,
Hopes that a breeze might lift it high.
While ants debate who's got the most,
In this leafy, laughing ghost.

Wind whispers secrets, soft and clear,
Laughter lingers, we endear.
Nature's chuckles fill the air,
A frolicking world beyond compare.

Harmonies of Life's Nourishing Touch

A carrot jokes with a beet so red,
'Let's do the veggie dance instead!'
While broccoli sings, 'I'm stout and proud!'
Potatoes cheer, they've drawn a crowd!

Bumblebees hum an offbeat song,
'Dance, little flowers, let's all get along!'
The rainbow-shaded tulip crew,
Swaps silly hats, as flowers do.

The sunbeam winks, a playful sight,
Chasing shadows, left and right.
"Oh dear worm, don't be so shy!
Come join us, give that wiggle a try!"

Even the raindrops tap a beat,
As puddles gather for a treat.
Nature's laughter, pure delight,
A funny fellowship, day and night.

The Narrative Symphony of Earth's Cores

Down below, the moles convene,
Planning pranks in earth so green.
'Let's plant a story, make it grand!'
A tale of roots, both thick and fanned.

'The rocks will roll, let's teach them jive!'
Said one small stone, oh so alive.
And up above, the trees partake,
With branches swaying, make no mistake.

The mushrooms skit like clumsy fools,
Cackling cheerfully, breaking rules.
While worms recite their nightly prose,
In grasses tall, where mischief flows.

Earth's core in laughter hums along,
Nature's orchestra, vibrant and strong.
With roots entwined and echoes clear,
The stories of life are made sincere.

The Dreams Borne on Nature's Breath

Clouds drift by, wearing fluffy hats,
While squirrels plot against the cats.
'What's that you say?' the breeze does tease,
A mischief-maker in the trees!

The daisies wink, their petals bright,
'Hey bumblebee, you dance just right!'
While butterflies flutter, colors true,
Exchanging recipes for the stew.

The crickets serenade the stars,
With chirpy tunes, they raise the bar.
And fireflies flicker, playful sparks,
Turning the night into a lark.

Nature giggles, tickled by the moon,
With little laughs that make us swoon.
In this world where joy is free,
Dreams are born on the breeze, you see!

The Undulating Tales of the Land

In the field, a cow wore shoes,
Her dance left the farmer in quite a snooze.
The hens clucked a tune, oh so spry,
While a goat made a hat with a pie.

A fox in a tux met a hedgehog quite grand,
They both tried to waltz but fell on the sand.
With laughter that echoed through tall grass and reeds,
Even the flowers were laughing at these misdeeds.

The sun tickled daisies, who giggled with glee,
While dandelions puffed up, oh so carefree.
A rabbit, a jester, jived near a fence,
Knocking over carrots, all dropping intense!

The ants threw a party with crumbs as the prize,
While the squirrels traded nuts with mischievous eyes.
Each critter contributed their quirkiest quirk,
In this land of laughter, nobody worked!

Harmonies in the Whispering Woods

A tree sang a tune to the breeze all day,
While the owls tried to rap in their sleepy way.
Beneath, the mushrooms played maracas with flair,
Creating a band that filled up the air.

A bear tried to dance but stepped on a bee,
That bee buzzed a rhythm, 'Now follow me!'
While the deer leapt around, trying out a twist,
All critters joined in, none wanting to miss.

The berries would giggle, ripe with a smile,
As the squirrels dressed up in fashion so vile.
A snail stole the show in a sparkly shell,
He twirled to the music and aimed to expel.

The breeze through the leaves played the funniest notes,
And the brook chimed in with bubbles and floats.
Together they crafted a lively parade,
In the woods' funny show that none would evade!

The Tides of Nature's Voice

The river splashed jokes to the stones on its way,
While frogs leaped with joy, croaking, 'Hip hip hooray!'
Fish twirled in circles, creating a scene,
A splash-tastic ballet, looking quite keen.

Tall grasses swayed, trying to do the cha-cha,
But a cheeky old turtle stole their bravura.
He spun on his shell, much to their surprise,
While dragonflies hovered, rolling their eyes.

A heron stood tall, wearing a silly hat,
As the turtles and frogs yelled, 'Now that's where it's at!'
The moon chuckled softly, watching their spree,
In the waves' swirling laughter, so wild and carefree.

The sun dipped down, painting the sky,
As the critters grew tired yet wished not to pry.
With a wave and a wink, the night took the stage,
And nature's fun tales turned the next page.

Rhymes from Beneath the Green Canopy

Below the broad leaves, a party took flight,
Where crickets recited their rhymes every night.
A worm with a mic rapped, living the dream,
While shades of the moon lit up the whole scene.

The bugs all gathered, drumming with zest,
While spiders spun webs for a sticky fest.
They boogied and bounced without any care,
As the fireflies twinkled, adding to flair.

The roots cheered them on with vibrations so low,
While the mushrooms hummed, just going with the flow.
A tortoise judged dance-offs with clever applause,
Making sure everyone followed the laws!

As dawn approached, they knew each bug knew,
Tomorrow would bring more backstage debut.
And so they all nestled, beneath the green dome,
In the rhythm of nature, forever their home.

Portraits in Petals and Leaves

In the garden, a bloom's big grin,
Waving petals, like a happy whim.
The dandelion, bold with pride,
Shouts, "I'm the king!" from its leafy ride.

Butterflies bust a move so tight,
While ladybugs dance in the sunlight.
A squirrel giggles, steals a seed,
Swears he's a foodie, in daredevil speed.

Sunflowers turn to face the crew,
As if they know just what to do.
They wink and laugh at clouds up high,
"Bring on the rain! We're all too shy!"

So play a tune on a flower's stem,
Nature's chorus, a wacky gem.
With every rustle, they disclose,
A joy so silly, the garden glows.

The Tapestry of Colorful Life

Colors clash, a vibrant brawl,
Roses with thorns, they've got the gall.
Bluebells chime in, "We've got flair!"
While sunflowers shout, "Who needs a hair?"

Bumblebees buzz, wearing their suits,
Dancing between the wild, fierce roots.
Daisies giggle, not a care in sight,
Pretending to nap, 'til the moon is bright.

Grasshoppers jump, in rhythm they play,
To the beat of nature, in a silly way!
"Catch me if you can!" they all tease,
Creating a ruckus, swaying with ease.

Then comes the wind, a joker sly,
Tickling the flowers, making them cry.
With laughter and whispers, life's sweet jest,
In this colorful tapestry, we're truly blessed.

Lyrics of the Gentle Earth

The ground hums a tune, soft and clear,
"Hey buddy, lend me your ear!"
Worms wiggling, singing with pride,
"Who needs a microphone? Just ride!"

Crickets chirp, with flair and rhythm,
Making beats as they dance in prism.
"Join us now in this merry song,
In fields of laughter, you can't go wrong!"

Flowers chime in, each with a tale,
"I'm the prettiest!" declares a snail.
With petals swinging in dapper grace,
Ready to waltz, all over the place!

The earth lets loose a delightful laugh,
While nature pens down its whimsical shaft.
With every rustling leaf and bark,
The lyrics of joy grow ever stark.

A Canvas of Whispering Wheat

Wheat waves hello in golden swirls,
"Watch me twirl!" as it giggles and whirls.
A scarecrow stands with a silly pose,
Pretending to be a bouquet of those!

The breeze whispers jokes to ears so tall,
While crickets sit back, enthralled by it all.
"Who needs a radio? Nature's the best,"
As each stalk dances, it's truly blessed.

A rabbit hops in, wearing a grin,
"Did you hear that one? Let's do it again!"
With laughter rippling in the field's embrace,
The canvas of wheat wears a comical face.

The sun sets low, paints a majestic show,
Laughing with colors as day starts to slow.
A masterpiece hung in the evening breeze,
Whispering life's humor, aiming to please.

Dialogues at Dusk's Horizon

Beneath the glow of twilight's gleam,
The flowers chuckle, quite the team.
A daisy tells a joke to thyme,
As crickets hum, they keep the rhyme.

A beetle rolls, with pride so grand,
Confessing tales of grains of sand.
The clouds above, they start to yawn,
While shadows stretch on waking dawn.

The grass, though still, can't hold its laugh,
As squirrels debate the perfect half.
A stork flies in, with wild intent,
To steal a joke that's heaven-sent.

And with each chat, more giggles rise,
Echoing through the starry skies.
In every rustle, chatter thrives,
Dusk brings forth, how laughter drives.

The Narrative of the Thistle

A thistle stood, all prickly wise,
Whispered tales with shifty eyes.
"I prickle hearts, don't be afraid,
I'm just the punchline, never played!"

Dandelions slept, their fluff on show,
"Why don't we fly?" a puffball said, though.
"Because," said one, "we've got our roots,
And flying close to ground's our hoots!"

They schemed of ways to make a scene,
A jest or two to cut routine.
A bee rolled by, with pollen sips,
"Is this a joke? Are you all quips?"

The thistle grinned, "We have much flair,
And laughter dances in the air.
Join us, friend, let's make a jest,
In this fine patch, we are the best!"

Quatrains from the Quaking Aspens

When whispers float from rallying leaves,
The quakies giggle, forget their grieves.
"We sway in rhythm, it's never a bore,
Whispering secrets from door to door!"

A squirrel makes faces, jumping around,
With acorn jokes that surely astound.
"Why do we play?" the branches tease,
"Because it's fun to dance with ease!"

The sun dips low, with rays that twirl,
Chasing light, the shadows whirl.
Every rustle brings a squeal of joy,
From every twig and playful ploy.

The achy trunks, with laughter sore,
Echo the giggles, never a chore.
In this forest, humor's like breeze,
With each wave, our hearts find ease.

Lullabies of the Grasshopper's Dance

In twilight's glow, the grasshoppers leap,
With little feet, they dare to creep.
"They say I'm loud, but it's just my song,
Come join the fun, you can't be wrong!"

The fireflies blink, a light parade,
Winking at every playful charade.
"Should we dance or should we chill?"
"Both, my friends, let's add some thrill!"

A ladybug, with polka-dot pride,
Joins the jig and can't abide.
"Why walk when we can hop around?
With every leap, new laughs are found!"

So as the night wraps its gentle shawl,
The insects gather, heeding the call.
The echoes blend with airy prance,
In quiet moments, joy finds its stance.

Whispers of the Wandering Wind

A gaggle of geese in flight,
Chasing after clouds so bright.
They squawk and honk, what a sight!
Wondering if they've lost their night.

Breeze tickles the grass, gives it a shake,
That's just the wind playing, for goodness' sake!
Whispers and giggles, a laugh we all make,
As flowers bloom, it's nature's cupcake.

A squirrel performs acrobatics up high,
With a nut in his paws, he leaps to the sky.
"I swear these branches are trampoline shy!"
He tells the bees, who just buzz and sigh.

So come, sit and watch this wild jamboree,
With chuckles and sighs, for all, it's free!
Nature's a comic, just look and you'll see,
Even the trees joke with glee on the spree.

Chronicles of the Small Creatures

A mouse with a hat is planning a feast,
With crumbs and cheese, he's quite the beast!
He invites the ants, they'll say the least,
"Don't forget the party hats, it's a great feast!"

A caterpillar with dreams of a winged spree,
Wonders aloud, "Will I fly, oh me?"
Then gets distracted by a bite of brie,
His hope takes a break, as snacks set him free.

Ants in a line, a well-practiced march,
They bump into each other, an overload larch.
"Move over, my friend, you're taking my starch!"
Laughter erupts, a comical parch.

With giggles and antics, the night wears thin,
As fireflies dance, with shimmering chin.
To the smallest of creatures, let the fun begin,
For laughter and joy is where we all win.

The Sun's Embrace and Earth's Response

The sun pops up with a wink and a ray,
"It's time to get up, no more delay!"
The flowers stretch out, they shout, "Hooray!"
But daisies trip over, "Whoops! Not today!"

A worm wakes up, in a snug little hole,
"It's getting too bright, I need my sun role!"
He twists and he turns, as warm vibes console,
"What's all this chatter? Is my name on a scroll?"

Grass blades giggle, whispering tales,
Of bees buzzing close with their pollen-filled pails.
"Are we in a cartoon? This feels like gales!"
"Oh yes!" chuckles Sun, "It is all in the scales!"

So under this warmth, the day dances free,
With laughter and pranks from each tiny bee.
The earth sings a tune, as it rolls in glee,
Embracing the antics of life's jubilee.

Glistening Tales of the Twilight

Twilight descends with a shimmer and glow,
Fireflies appear, they put on a show.
"Do you see me dance?" They flicker and flow,
While crickets chime in, "To the beat, let's go!"

A toad jumps in, with a croak and a cheer,
"Keep time with my leaps, oh let's make it clear!"
While bugs all around spin tales that we hear,
Of romance with moonbeams, a party of sheer.

In the coolness that settles, a fox struts along,
Whispering secrets to the night's sweet song.
"Please, dear stars, join us, don't take too long,
For laughter awaits where all of us throng!"

As twinkling starlight joins in the jest,
The night grows alive, putting all to the test.
With nocturnal laughter, they throw a grand fest,
In the twilight's embrace, where fun is the best.

www.ingramcontent.com/pod-product-compliance
Lightning Source LLC
Chambersburg PA
CBHW051633160426
43209CB00004B/635